THEN AND THERE SERIES
GENERAL EDITOR
MARJORIE REEVES, M.A., PH.D.

Captain Cook and the Pacific

DAVID W. SYLVESTER

Illustrated from contemporary sources

LONGMAN

D1343921

LONGMAN GROUP LIMITED
London
Associated companies, branches and representatives throughout the world

ⓒ *Longman Group Ltd 1971*

First published 1971
ISBN 0 582 20462 3

Acknowledgements
We are grateful to the following for permission to reproduce copyright material:
The editor and Angus and Robertson Limited for extracts from *The Endeavour
Journal of Joseph Banks 1768–1771* edited by J. C. Beaglehole; the editor, the
Hakluyt Society and the Cambridge University Press for extracts from
The Journals of Captain Cook edited by J. C. Beaglehole.
For permission to reproduce photographs we are grateful to the following:
Bernice P. Bishop Museum, page 83; Earl of Birkenhead, page 67; British
Museum, pages 5, 27 *(right)*, 32, 33, 37 *(top* and *bottom)*, 39, 41 *(top* and *bottom)*,
46, 47, 48, 49 *(left* and *right)*, 50, 60, 79; British Museum (Natural History),
pages 29, 34, 52, 56; Mitchell Library, New South Wales, pages 21 *(left)*, 68;
National Maritime Museum, Greenwich, pages 8, 15, 16, 19, 64, 73; Peabody
Museum, Harvard University, pages 80, 81 *(top* and *bottom)*, the Hon. Mrs. Clive
Pearson, Parham Park, Sussex, page 23; Public Archives of Canada, page 72;
The Sutcliffe Gallery, page 87.
The maps on pages 43, 55, and 62/63 were redrawn from the *Journals of Captain
Cook*, edited by J. C. Beaglehole, Cambridge University Press for the Hakluyt
Society, 1967; page 20 was reproduced and the map on page 86 was redrawn from
Captain Cook by Alan Villiers, Hodder and Stoughton, 1967; page 74 was redrawn
from *Cook and the opening of the Pacific* by J. A. Williamson, Edinburgh University
Press, 1946, ⓒ George Philip & Son Ltd.

Printed in Hong Kong by Yu Luen Offset Printing Factory

Contents

To the Reader

'Adventure', 'Discovery', 'Endeavour' and 'Resolution'—these are the names of Captain Cook's ships. They also tell you what this book is about.

It is not easy to get to know Captain James Cook. For we have no long descriptions of him as a person, left by people who knew him. Nor do his portraits help much for they are all very different, as you will see when you look at those on pages 16 and 64.

However we do have Cook's own Journals in which he kept a record of his three great voyages in the Pacific Ocean. These have been edited by a great scholar, Professor J. C. Beaglehole of the Victoria University of Wellington, New Zealand, and this book is based on them. Together with other journals kept by some of those who went with Cook we can find out in great detail what Cook did. And in reading about what he did we can discover what sort of man he was.

Words printed in *italics* are explained in the Glossary (p. 90).

1 The Royal Society

On 15 February 1768 a group of learned gentlemen gathered in London for a meeting of the Council of the Royal Society. This was to be a very important meeting, for the Fellows of the Royal Society had been discussing certain matters for the past eighteen months and now was the day for decision.

The Royal Society had been founded more than a hundred years previously in 1662 when Charles II had become its royal patron. It existed to encourage study in the various sciences and only those who showed a real knowledge of these subjects were elected Fellows. Today the Royal Society still exists and to be elected one of its Fellows is one of the greatest honours a scientist can achieve. Most of the Fellows nowadays are professional scientists who can earn their living by their studies in science at the universities or in other centres of scientific research. In the eighteenth century most of the Fellows were *amateur* scientists who did not earn money from their studies but who studied in their spare time because they found science interesting. Some of the Fellows were country clergymen, some were bishops, some were gentlemen living off small country estates and some were very rich lords, some were scholars from the Universities of Oxford and Cambridge, but all were interested in scientific experiments and discoveries.

On this particular day the Council of the Royal Society were concerned with one branch of science, *astronomy*. It was known that in 1769 the planet Venus would pass across the face of the sun. This was a rare event and the Royal Society wanted to make sure that this 'Transit of Venus', as it is called, was properly observed and noted. For if accurate observations of the *transit* were taken from different points on the earth's surface, astronomers would be able to calculate the distance of the earth from the sun. It had first been observed in 1639 by a young parson, Jeremiah Horrocks, who lived at Hoole in Lancashire. Then Edmund Halley who was the Astronomer Royal from 1720 to 1742, calculated that it would occur again in 1761 and also in 1769. After that it would not be seen until 1874. In 1761 British scientists had tried to make observations of the transit but they had not been very successful. One observer had been sent to St Helena but on the day of the transit it had been cloudy there and little had been seen. Others had been sent to Sumatra but had never reached it and though they had landed at the Cape of Good Hope they had not been able to make good observations. The Royal Society were determined not to lose their opportunity in 1769. As early as 5 June 1766 they 'resolved to send astronomers to several parts of the World in order to Observe the Transit'. In November 1767 the Society appointed a committee to make its plans. After many calculations the committee reported that for the best set of observations, some observers should be sent north, to the North Cape of Norway and to Fort Churchill in Hudson Bay, and others south, preferably to an island in the Pacific Ocean half-way between Chile and the Dutch Indies and between the Equator and 20°S.

The Royal Society accepted these suggestions but where was the money to come from for the expeditions? The Society hoped that the Hudson's Bay Company would take observers to Fort Churchill in one of their ships. They hoped also to be able to send an observer to the North Cape on the naval vessel which went there every year to protect the fisheries. The main problem was the expedition to the Pacific and this was what the Council of the Royal Society met to consider on 15 February 1768. At that meeting it decided to appeal to the government for money and it signed and sent the following *memorial* to the King.

'Humbly sheweth—That the passage of the Planet Venus over the Disc of the Sun, which will happen on the 3rd of

June in the year 1769, is a *Phaenomenon* that must, if the same be accurately observed in proper places, contribute greatly to the improvement of Astronomy on which navigation so much depends. . . . That the like appearance after the 3rd of June 1769 will not happen for more than 100 years. . . . That the British Nation have been justly celebrated in the learned world for their knowledge of Astronomy in which they are *inferior* to no Nation upon Earth . . . and it would cast dishonour upon them should they neglect to have correct Observations made of this important Phaenomenon. . . . That a correct Set of Observations made in a Southern Latitude would be of greater importance than many of those made in the Northern. . . . That the expence of having the Observations properly made in the Places above specified (the North Cape, Fort Churchill, the South Seas) including a reasonable *gratification* to the persons employed, and furnishing them with such Instruments as are still wanting, would amount to about 4000 pounds, exclusive of the expence of the ships which must convey and return Observers to the Southwards of the *Equinoctial* Line and to the North Cape. That the Royal Society are in no condition to *defray* this Expence. . . . The Memorialists, attentive to the true end for which they were founded by your Majesty's Royal Predecessor, the Improvement of Natural Knowledge, conceive it to be their duty to lay these *sentiments* before your Majesty with all humility and submit the same for your Majesty's Royal consideration.

King George III was quick to reply. He was always ready to help new projects and by 5 March 1768 the Royal Society had been promised £4,000 and the Admiralty had been ordered to provide a ship for the expedition to the Pacific.

2   The Unknown Southern Continent

As preparations for the expedition went ahead it became clear that as well as the observation of Venus there were other aims in view.

First, many Fellows of the Royal Society, and others too, hoped that the expedition would increase geographical knowledge. Geographical exploration was one of the great interests of the eighteenth century. In the same way that we today are very interested in space exploration, so the people of those days were interested in the exploration of the world. Since about 1690 many travel books had been published in England and they were the most popular books of those times. If you had looked at the great library of a Lord's mansion you would have found travel books there. If you had gone around the smaller country houses of the landed gentlemen of England you would have found the large *folios* and *quartos* of travel books on their shelves. You would have found other copies in clergymen's houses up and down the countryside and also in towns in the houses of merchants and customs officials. Travel books were best sellers. William Dampier's 'New Voyage round the World' published in 1697 was a great favourite and the 'Complete Collection of Voyages or Travels' edited by Dr John Campbell between 1744 and 1748 was another.

The reason for all this interest in geography in the eighteenth century was that there was still so much to discover. In some ways men knew no more than the geographers of the ancient world. They had argued that since the earth was a sphere and that in the northern half of it there were the three land

continents of Europe, Asia and Africa, then there was likely to

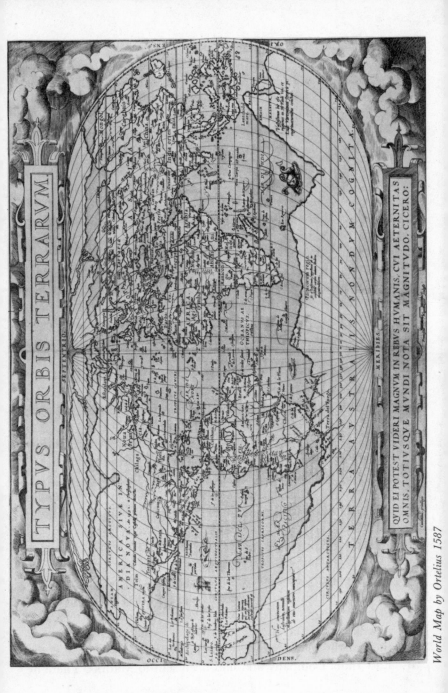

World Map by Ortelius 1587

be land in its southern half to act as a balance. So they believed that somewhere in the ocean to the south was a vast continent which they called in Latin 'Terra Australis Incognita'—the 'Unknown Southern Land'. Men still believed this in the eighteenth century and their picture of the world was very much like that shown by the Flemish geographer Abraham Ortelius in his World-Map of 1587. You can see it on page 5. This map shows the continent of America and this was something which the ancient geographers had not known about. It also shows the Mar del Zur, the 'South Sea' as the Spaniard Balboa called it when he first saw it after struggling across the isthmus of Panama in 1513. Seven years later Magellan found a passage from the Atlantic through South America into the South Sea, but he called it the Pacific and this is the name that has survived. As you can see, Ortelius puts both names upon his map. Since Ortelius there had been several attempts by sailors from different European nations to find out more about the Pacific and what land it contained. The Dutch discovered Western Australia and called it New Holland. In a voyage beginning in 1642 Abel Tasman, another Dutchman, went further south and discovered Tasmania and the west coast of New Zealand which he called Staten Land. New Guinea was well known though it was not clear whether it was the northern part of Australia or not. In fact a Portuguese, Luis Vaez de Torres, had sailed through the straits south of New Guinea in 1605, but his discovery that New Guinea was an island was not made public. By 1700 various other islands had been sighted and named, but the riddle of the Pacific remained unanswered. Was there 'Terra Australis Incognita'?

At least one Fellow of the Royal Society believed very strongly that there was such a continent in the South. This was Alexander Dalrymple. Not only did he hope like many other people that this expedition to the Pacific would discover vast new lands, but he also hoped that he would be chosen to lead the expedition. Born in 1737 he had entered the service of the East India Company and had been sent to Madras. There he became very interested in voyages of discovery. He taught himself surveying, navigation and astronomy and went to sea in command of one of the Company's merchant ships. He studied all that he could find about voyages in the Pacific and he even discovered an account of the voyage of Torres which showed that a strait existed between New Guinea and Australia. It was the first time that the existence of Torres Strait had been brought to light. When Dalrymple came back to England in 1765 he wrote 'An Account of the Discoveries made in the South Pacific Ocean Previous to 1764', though he did not publish it until 1769. In 1770–1771 he brought out two volumes of his 'Collection of Voyages to the South Seas' and he made his belief in a Southern Continent quite clear. He wrote:

'It cannot be doubted . . . that the SOUTHERN CONTINENT has been already discovered on the east side; and it appears more than probable that Tasman's discovery, which he named STAAT'S LAND, but which is in the maps called NEW ZEALAND, is the western coast of this Continent. . . . The number of inhabitants in the Southern Continent is probably more than 50 millions. . . .'

It is not suprising that the Council of the Royal Society should suggest Mr Dalrymple as the commander of the expedition, he 'having a particular turn for discoveries and being an able navigator and well skilled in observation'. However, it was up to the Lords of the *Admiralty* to decide upon a commander, and they thought differently from the Royal Society.

The Admiralty were not as concerned about observing Venus or increasing geographical knowledge as the Fellows of the Royal Society. They wanted to discover new lands and continents for political reasons. They saw it as part of the race to obtain a bigger and better empire than that of the Spanish or the French. They had fought for the trade of the Spanish Empire in the War of Spanish Succession 1701–14, and they had fought the French for the riches of India and North America in the Seven Years War 1756–63. Sending out expeditions to find new lands was for the Lords of the Admir- 7

Alexander Dalrymple

alty just another way of continuing the struggle. Since the beginning of the eighteenth century they had sent out such expeditions. In 1699 the Admiralty sent William Dampier to the Pacific and he had come back with a glowing account of the trade possibilities of New Britain which he had discovered and named. In 1740 Commodore Anson was sent to stir up the peoples in Chile and Peru to break away from the Spanish

Empire and also to investigate the Falkland Isles as a possible British base. The Cape Horn passage battered his ships so that he achieved little but he did make one raid at Paita on the coast of Peru and he captured a Spanish treasure ship worth over £600,000 before crossing the Pacific and returning to England in 1744. In 1764 Commodore Byron was sent to investigate the Falklands once again, and his other orders were to enter the Pacific and then sail north in search of the North-West passage from the Pacific to Hudson Bay which many still thought might exist. Byron charted the north coast of the Falklands but then struck across the Pacific and arrived home in May 1766. He had gained a base for the British in the Falklands but as a voyage of discovery it had achieved nothing. In the same year that Byron came home, the British Government sent Captain Samuel Wallis in the same ship that Byron had used, the 'Dolphin', to search for a southern continent and claim it in the name of the King of Great Britain. He rounded the Horn but then winds drove him northwards, and though he discovered Tahiti and spent a delightful week there being entertained by friendly natives, when he returned home the riddle of the Pacific was still unsolved. From all this it is clear that the Admiralty were as eager to send an expedition to the Pacific as the Royal Society. But this time they wanted it to be a successful expedition and so they thought for a long time before choosing its commander.

The Admiralty did not like the idea of having non-naval men to command naval vessels. They remembered that in 1698 the astronomer Edmund Halley had been given command of the naval vessel 'Paramour Pink' so that he could make studies on the compass, but he had failed to control his crew and had been forced to give up his voyage. As Hawke, the First Sea Lord said, 'he would suffer his right hand to be cut off' rather than agree to such a commander again. So early in April 1768 they told the Royal Society that they could not commission Mr Dalrymple as commander of the expedition as it 'was totally *repugnant* to the rules of the navy'. Instead they appointed Mr James Cook, then master of the schooner 'Grenville'. 9

3   Lieutenant James Cook, R.N.

The first thing people noticed about James Cook was his size. He was over six feet high and he carried himself erect like a soldier. He was now forty years old and his life so far had been a varied and eventful one.

He was born at Marton in Yorkshire on 27 October 1728. His father, also James Cook, was a farm labourer, but shortly after his son's birth he became foreman on the nearby farm of Mr Thomas Scottowe at Great Ayton. Here James Cook passed his boyhood, going to school when he was eight with his father's employer paying the school fees. He could read already but at school he learned writing and arithmetic. He probably left school early and then he worked until he was seventeen on the farm. His father thought that he would do better for himself in life if he left farm work so, in 1745, James was sent to the village of Staithes on the Yorkshire coast to learn how to run a general store. His new employer, Mr Saunderson, had a good grocery and drapery business and here James Cook began to learn the 'trade'. It was unusual in the eighteenth century for a farm labourer's son to learn enough of the three 'Rs'—reading, writing and 'rithmetic—to be able to leave the land and enter business. James Cook was lucky. Yet he was not satisfied. At Staithes he breathed the sea air and began to think that life on a ship would be far more exciting than in a shop. He talked about it with his employer, Mr Saunderson, and the shopkeeper agreed to introduce him to some ship-owning friends of his in Whitby. James Cook went to see them. They were two elderly *Quaker* brothers called Walker and their house in Grape Lane, Whitby, still stands.

James Cook's cottage at Great Ayton, now in Fitzroy Gardens, Melbourne, Australia

At first they were not very eager to take Cook. Most *apprentices* came to them when they were fourteen and did seven full years before they were passed out as able seamen. Cook was already eighteen and though he seemed clever and a good worker they wondered if he could learn all that had to be learned in the three years before he was twenty-one. On the other hand few boys in those days would deliberately choose to be a sailor for the life was a hard one. Yet Cook was throwing up the respectable trade of shopkeeper because he had decided that above all things he wanted to go to sea. This, in the end, 11 convinced the Walker brothers and in July 1746 Cook became their apprentice.

The family firm of John Walker of Whitby was mainly engaged in shipping coal from Northumberland to London. Almost immediately Cook found himself one of half a dozen apprentices on board the 'Freelove'. This was a ship of 450 tons, typical of those built at Whitby and known to seafaring folk as a 'cat'. This name describes the shape of the hull of these ships which with the two *hawseholes* cut in its 'face' made it look a little like a cat. The Whitby cats were very strongly built ships with large *holds* for their cargoes of coal. They were of small *draught* so that they could work in the shallow waters and harbours of the coast, and though not fast they were very reliable. The quarters for the crew were cramped and Cook found that his six feet of height meant that he banged his head frequently until he got used to the small headroom. But at last he was doing what he wanted to do and he made sure that he learned as much as he could in the quickest time possible.

During the winter months he lived with the Walkers in their house and worked hard at his mathematics and navigation. He also helped in the repair work on the ships, for during the times of bad weather between Christmas and March the ships were thoroughly overhauled. Their rigging was stored away in lofts, sails were sent off to the sailmakers, the hulls were *fumigated* and any holes in the woodwork both on deck and below were made good.

In March the coal-carrying trade to London began again. It was an excellent training for Cook and especially helpful to him in his later career of exploring uncharted coasts. The voyage to London lay through shallow coastal waters, sandbanks, fast currents and changing tides. There were no lighthouses to guide the sailors, though on some headlands coal fires were kept burning in *braziers* as a warning light. Cook learned to recognise the channels between the sandbanks and the local landmarks. As one of the apprentices, it was often his job to swing the *lead* into the sea, calculate from the length of

12   wet leadline how deep the water was, and then shout it out to

Names of Officers and Seamen.	Post on Board.	Age.	Where born, and Place of Abode.		Name of Ship, and Master, and what Voyage each Man last performed.
			Birth.	Abode.	
19	Richard Ellerton	Mas	Whitby	Ayton	Constant Mary Nicholas Jackson
	James Cook	Mate		Whitby	Three Brothers
	James Dale	Carp:		D:	
	Francis Rice	Cook		D:	
	John Founder	Seaman			

Entry of James Cook as Mate in Muster Roll of the 'Friendship'

the Mate of the ship. For three hard years he learned the seaman's business: how to man the *windlass* or the *capstan*, how to get up aloft, how to furl the sails. For three more years he served as an able seaman, and then in 1752 he was promoted Mate. The Walkers were well pleased with the way in which their apprentice had turned out. If he continued to serve them well in three or four years he was likely to become captain of a Whitby 'cat'.

Cook did continue to do well. In the summer of 1755 he was Mate of the 'cat' 'Friendship' taking coal to London and he had been told that when he returned to Whitby after this voyage he would be offered command of the ship. At twenty-seven years of age his future seemed clear. Cook, however, decided otherwise. War between England and France was brewing and as Cook steered the 'Friendship' up the Thames and saw the ships-of-war being fitted out, he 'had a mind to try his fortune that way'.

With war coming there was a 'hot press' in all the seaports. In other words the navy wanted more men and they used press-gangs to force men, whether landsmen or merchant seamen, into their service. Cook, as the master of a merchantman, was exempt from *impressment*, so he had no need to join the navy, unless he wanted to. This was what he did want. The war offered him a life wider than that of the North Sea and on 17 June 1755 he volunteered at Wapping as an Able Seaman. He was sent to the 60-gun ship 'Eagle' at Portsmouth on 25 June, and so he began his career in the Royal Navy.

13

For the next two years, 1755–57, the 'Eagle' helped to blockade the French coast and this meant that she cruised up and down the Channel chasing and stopping vessels suspected of supplying the French. Cook soon showed his abilities and within a month he was made master's mate. Within another six months he became *boatswain* and so had command of the *cutter* which did much of the chasing of suspected vessels. Once he was given charge of a captured vessel and had the job of sailing her up the Thames to London. During this time he was under the command of Captain Hugh Palliser, another Yorkshireman. Palliser saw how able Cook was and he decided to recommend him for promotion. In July 1757, Cook was promoted to master and he joined the 'Pembroke', a ship of 64 guns. The master was an officer whose main duty was to be in charge of navigation. It was a very important position.

In February 1758 the 'Pembroke' crossed the Atlantic, as one of the fleet under Admiral Boscawen, which carried the 14,000 strong army of Colonel Amherst to North America. William Pitt had just become leader of the British in their war against the French and this expedition was part of his plan to drive the French out of Canada. First the British captured Louisbourg after a long seige and then they went back to Halifax for the winter. Next year, in 1759, the British began the move up the St Lawrence to capture Quebec. It was difficult to sail up the St Lawrence for it was a fast-flowing river. Yet the British plan was to sail their largest ships up the river so that they could bombard Quebec with their guns. The job of finding a safe passage for the ships was given to the master of the 'Pembroke'. Working at night under cover of the dark, Cook with the other masters and sailors *sounded* and then charted these difficult waters, which were full of rocks and *shoals*. It was a long tiring job, but it had its reward, for in September 1759 the fleet sailed safely up to Quebec and James Wolfe was able to lead his men up the cliffs and so capture the French fort. The French had lost Canada. You can read more about the capture of Quebec in the 'Then and There' book,

'The Struggle for Canada'.

Captain Hugh Palliser

After this Cook became master on the 'Northumberland', the flagship of rear-admiral Lord Colville, who was now commander-in-chief in North American waters. Cook continued to survey the St Lawrence and the coasts of Nova Scotia and Newfoundland, and his charts were published and became the standard maps of those waters for the next hundred years. In 1762, while on leave in England, Cook married Elizabeth Batts, the daughter of a family of craftsmen who lived near the Thames in London. I wonder if she knew what sort of a life she would have being married to a sailor who was to be away at sea for most of the seventeen years of their married life? Cook was only at home for four months before he was away again for five years surveying the Newfoundland waters for the benefit of the fishing and naval fleets. In 1764,   15

James Cook by Nathaniel Danco

though he remained a master, he got his own ship to command, the schooner 'Grenville'. In the autumn of 1764 Cook had a slight accident when a powder-horn exploded in his right hand. It left scars but Cook could still use his hand. In winter he used to sail the 'Grenville' back to England and lay her up for the winter while he worked at home on his charts. Then in spring off he would go for more surveying work. In the winter of 1767–8 Cook was back in London as usual. In the spring he began to fit out the 'Grenville' ready for her return to Newfoundland, but when the ship sailed, it was without Cook.

The Admiralty had been pleased with his work of the past ten years. In 1762 when Cook was beginning to publish his charts, Lord Colville, his commander, had written to the Admiralty about 'Mr Cook's genius and capacity' and had said 'I think him well qualified for the work he has performed and for greater undertakings of the same kind.' Since 1764 Palliser had been commander in Newfoundland waters and he also spoke highly of Mr Cook to the Admiralty. Moreover, Palliser was now at the Navy Board as *comptroller*. It was not surprising then that the Admiralty should select James Cook to command the expedition to the Pacific and *commission* him as lieutenant.

When the Royal Society heard the decision, Mr Dalrymple was very annoyed and refused to go on the expedition even as an observer, but the Council were quite happy. Mr Cook was known to them, for in 1766 he had made observations of an *eclipse* of the sun in Newfoundland and his report had been published in the 'Transactions' of the Royal Society. It seemed to the Council that Cook was well qualified to be one of the observers they wished to send to the Pacific and they offered the position to him. On 19 May 1768 Cook accepted the position and the fee of one hundred guineas which went along with it. He was now, together with a Mr Green, an official observer for the Royal Society of the Transit of Venus due to take place in 1769. He was also commander of His Majesty's ship the 'Endeavour', now being fitted out at Deptford.

4   The 'Endeavour'

The Admiralty had been looking for a suitable ship for the expedition since the beginning of March 1768. They sent their officials to report on various vessels and in the end they chose a Whitby 'cat', the 'Earl of Pembroke'. She was three years nine months old and had been used as a *collier* in the trade up and down the east coast. Her owner was a Mr Thomas Milner and the Admiralty bought her from him for £2,800. By 5 April 1768 the Admiralty had given orders for her to be fitted out at Deptford for service in the Pacific and to be registered on the List of the Navy as a *bark* by the name of the 'Endeavour'.

The 'Endeavour' is one of the best known ships in history for we have official records of her body-plan, her masts and many of her fittings. She was 368 tons, 106 feet long and 29 feet 3 inches broad at her furthest points. She was not a large ship but ideal for exploration, since she was of moderate draught and strongly constructed to withstand running aground. There was room, too, in her hold for plenty of stores. However, various alterations were needed before she was fit to sail to the Pacific.

On 22 April 1768 John Satterley was appointed carpenter of the 'Endeavour'. Soon after, gangs of joiners were to be seen boarding the ship every day to work under Satterley on the job of refitting. The first and most important job was to provide the 'Endeavour' with protection against the borer-worms which would swarm to attack her when she reached the warm waters of the Tropics. These worms bored into the planks of a ship and then began to eat their way through them, all the time breeding more and more worms until in the end the

'Endeavour', (model) National Maritime Museum

whole of the hull was ready to crumble. Experiments had been made to *sheathe* the bottom of ships with copper as a protection against these worms. The 'Dolphin' in which Wallis had sailed to the Pacific in 1766 had been sheathed with copper. The experiments were not completely successful. The copper was thin and easily damaged and it was hard to repair when a ship was a long way from home. It was decided that the 'Endeavour' should have the more usual type of protection. The underwater parts of the ship were covered with a layer of tarred felt and then an outer skin of planks was nailed on with thousands of flat-headed nails set as close together as possible. The next job was to renew the masts and yards for most of them were found to be faulty. The 'Endeavour' was rigged on three masts. The fore-mast and the main-mast both consisted of three sections: lower-mast, topmast and topgallant, and they were rigged with sails on each section. The mizzen-mast was shorter and was rigged with sails on two sections only, the lower-mast and the topmast. (See the diagram). Another job was to fit her to carry guns and the 'Endeavour' eventually sailed with ten carriage guns and twelve *swivel* guns. Then 19

Sails and Rigging

A Jib
B Fore topmast staysail
C Spritsail
D Fore topgallantsail
E Fore topsail
F Foresail (or fore course)
G Main topgallant staysail
H Main topmast staysail
I Main topgallantsail
J Main topsail
K Mainsail (or main course)
L Mizzen topsail
M Spanker

N Fore-mast
O Main-mast
P Mizzen-mast
Q Jibboom (protruding beyond the bowsprit)
R Spritsail-yard
S Reef-points (used to gather up reefs, or tucks, in the sails)
T Braces (each yard has a pair, which lead to the deck)
U Bowlines (used to make the sails set better)

Braces and bowlines etc. take their precise names from the sails or yards they serve: e.g., the T on *the right* is the starboard fore topgallant brace. As the sails are set, it is also the lee fore topgallant brace, because it is on the lee side. The other side is then called the weather.

cabins had to be made for the officers and scientists. More store-rooms had to be found to hold enough provisions for a two-year voyage, and a bigger and better *galley* than that which a 'cat' usually carried, was built. On deck *stowages* had to be made for three new ship's boats: a *pinnace* was bought for Cook's own use as commander, a longboat was provided for carrying stores and finally, the smallest of the three, there was a *yawl*, which could be used to carry small parties of men. When all these jobs were done the ship was finished with a coat of pine varnish and her *spars* were painted black.

Soon stores were being loaded on to the 'Endeavour'. For example, on 15 June the Victualling Board gave the following orders.

'Lieut. James Cook, Endeavour *bark*, Deptford. Let the following provisions be sent to the said Bark, as desired, viz.

Bread in Bags 21,226 pounds
Ditto in Butts, 13,440 pounds
Flour for Bread in Barrells 9,000 pounds
Beer, in *Puncheons* 1,200 gallons
Spirits 1,600 gallons
Beef 4,000 pieces
Suet 800 pounds
Raisins 2,500 pounds
Pease in Butts 187 Bushells
Oatmeal 10 Bushells
Wheat 120 Bushells
Oil 120 gallons
Sugar 1,500 pounds
Vinegar 500 gallons
Sour Krout (pickled Cabbage) 7,860 pounds
Malt in Hogsheads 40 Bushells
Salt 20 ditto
Pork 6,000 pieces
Mustard seed 160 pounds'

Then there were supplies sent on board for the use of the Surgeon. The Admiralty were very concerned to try to find a cure for scurvy, that terrible disease which played havoc with the health of sailors who were at sea for any length of time. The symptoms were horrible: swellings on the body, bleeding gums and teeth dropping out, and shortness of breath. To try to prevent Cook's crew falling foul of scurvy the Admiralty sent on board juice of lemons and oranges 'to make trial of their *efficacy* in curing Scurvy' and also a special soup which was to be served with *pease* and oatmeal on Banyan days 'it having been found extremely beneficial in long voyages'. Banyan days were the three meatless days in the

Navy, namely Monday, Wednesday, and Friday. It was to be the Surgeon's job to make sure this juice and the soup were properly administered.

All this loading of stores and the refitting of the ship took time and money. When Cook had taken command of the 'Endeavour' on 27 May 1768 he had been ordered 'to make the utmost dispatch in getting her ready for the sea'. Cook tried to hurry things but it was not until 21 July that she left the dock at Deptford. Meanwhile the refitting alone, apart from the stores, had cost the Admiralty a lot of money, as the following figures make clear:

For work on hull, masts and yards, materials	£1,357 17s 11d
For work on hull, masts and yards, labour	935 19s 8d
For furnishings and carpenter's stores, materials	£3,043 11s 2d
For furnishings and carpenter's stores, labour	57 6s 7d

On top of the purchase price of £2,800 and the cost of the ship's boats, it made the 'Endeavour' an expensive ship.

As Cook sailed from Deptford he must have felt glad that most of the preparations were now done. He had orders to sail to Plymouth, there to receive final orders before the voyage began. Alas, it was not to be as simple as that. For the day after he sailed from Deptford he received the following order: 'You are hereby required and directed to receive on board . . . Joseph Banks Esq. and his Suite consisting of eight Persons with their baggage.' This meant that more cabins would have to be provided and when the 'Endeavour' arrived at Plymouth on 14 August it was once again boarded by ship-wrights and joiners to make the necessary alterations, all at extra cost.

Joseph Banks was a wealthy young man, twenty-four years old and the owner of large estates in Lincolnshire which brought him an income of £6,000 a year. While at school at Eton he had become very interested in *botany*. In fact he

Joseph Banks by Sir Joshua Reynolds

became so interested that when he went later to Oxford University and found that there was no one to teach him botany, he arranged for a lecturer to come over to him from Cambridge. After leaving the university he continued his botanical interests and in April 1766 he was elected a Fellow of the Royal Society. Soon after he joined H.M.S. 'Niger' bound for service in Newfoundland waters and Banks spent the rest of that year collecting plant specimens before returning to England in January 1767. After making a tour of the West of England he began looking for further opportunities to travel and the more he heard about the proposed voyage to the Pacific, the more it attracted him. If it was to be a voyage to increase man's knowledge of geography and astronomy, why not botany as well? Banks began to get in touch with all his influential friends, particularly the Earl of Sandwich who was a member of the Government. He also persuaded the Royal Society to write to the Admiralty requesting that he could join the expedition. As a result Joseph Banks, Esq., Fellow of the Royal Society, 'a Gentleman of Large Fortune,

23

well versed in Natural History' joined the 'Endeavour' at Plymouth.

Banks did not come alone. Also in the party was a Swedish botanist, Doctor Daniel Carl Solander and another Swedish naturalist Herman Spöring. There were two artists: Sydney Parkinson, a botanical draftsman, and Alexander Buchan who was engaged to do the *landscape* and figure drawing. There were two servants from the Banks' estates in Lincolnshire, named James Roberts and Peter Briscoe, and two other Negro servants, Thomas Richmond and George Dorlton. With them there were piles of baggage. Artists' and botanists' materials, enough to last for two years; canvases, easels, brushes, paints, books and writing materials, presses for plants, nets and hooks for fishing. There were bags full of clothes and personal things, and last but not least, there were two large greyhounds.

It was a problem to know where to put them all, for the 'Endeavour' was already an overcrowded ship with a crew of eighty-five, made up of officers, sailors and marines. Then there was the Royal Society's official observer, Charles Green and his servant John Reynolds, and now Joseph Banks and his party of eight. Had the additional voyagers been ordinary seamen they could have been given a hammock each and told to sling it as best they could on the lower deck. However, since they were 'civilians' cabins had to be found for them. In the end the problem was solved by letting Mr Banks' party take over the ship's officers' cabins and shifting the officers into small stuffy cabins on the lower deck.

These alterations to the cabins and the stowing aboard of more stores took twelve days. Then on 26 August 1768 the voyage began. Cook made the following entry in his Journal:

'Friday 26th. First part fresh breeze and Clowdy, remainder little wind and Clear. At 2 pm got under sail and put to sea having on board 94 persons including Officers Seamen Gentlemen and their servants, near 18 months provisions, 10 Carriage guns 12 Swivels with good store of Ammunition and stores of all kinds.'

1 First Lieutenant, James Cook
    and 1 Servant, William Howson
1 Second Lieutenant, Zachary Hickes
    and 1 Servant, William Harvey
1 Third Lieutenant, John Gore
    and 1 Servant, Nathaniel Morey
1 Master, Robert Molyneux
    and 1 Servant, Isaac Manley
1 Boatswain, John Gathrey
    and 1 Servant, Thomas Jordan
1 Gunner, Stephen Forwood
    and 1 Servant, Daniel Roberts
1 Carpenter, John Satterley
    and 1 Servant, Edward Terrell
1 Surgeon, William Monkhouse
    and 1 Servant, Thomas Jones
1 Cook, John Thompson
    and 1 Servant, Thomas Matthews
2 Masters Mates, Charles Clerke, Francis Wilkinson
3 Midshipmen, John Bootie, Jonathan Monkhouse, Patrick
    Saunders
1 Surgeon's Mate, William Perry
1 Clerk and Steward, Richard Orton
2 Quarter Masters, Alexander Weir, Samuel Evans
2 Boatswain's Mates, John Reading, Thomas Hardman
1 Carpenter's Mate, Richard Hughes
1 Armourer, Robert Taylor
1 Sailmaker, John Ravenhill
41 Able Seamen*
12 Marines, under Sergeant John Edgcumbe

*In fact there were only 39 seamen, for under a naval rule the captain of every ship which had a complement between 75 and 125, was allowed to count two extra *fictitious* seamen on his pay roll. These men were known as 'widow's men', for their pay went into the widows' pensions fund.

5 Observing Venus

The first part of the voyage lay on a route that was then well known: out of the Channel and across the Bay of Biscay, then south towards Madeira, where they hoped to meet the north-east 'trade winds' which would blow them across the Atlantic towards Rio de Janeiro. After that, the ship would have to sail down the coast of South America and round Cape Horn into the Pacific.

Joseph Banks and his party of naturalists and artists began their work as soon as the ship was clear of the land. Using a small casting net they landed various specimens of sea insects and crabs and Parkinson set to work to draw them. Then on the fourth day out the sea became heavier and Banks had a particularly bad bout of sea sickness which he recorded in his Journal.

'Aug. 29. Wind foul: Morning employed in finishing the Drawings of the animals taken yesterday till the ship got so much motion that Mr Parkinson could not set to his Pencil; in the Evening wind still Fresher so much as to make the night very uncomfortable.

30. Wind still Foul, ship in violent motion, but towards Evening much more quiet: Now for the first time my Sea sickness left me, and I was sufficiently well to write.'

In the days that followed Banks wrote more and more, filling his Journal with descriptions of their discoveries of the life that teemed in the sea and hoping that 'as Dr Solander and myself shall have probably greater opportunity in the

Dr Solander

Sydney Parkinson

course of this voyage than any one has had before us . . . we may be able . . . to add considerable light to the science which we so eagerly pursue.'

The 'Endeavour' put in at Madeira on 13 September. This was a necessary call for since neither water nor beer would keep for very long without going foul, ships usually took on fresh water here and also stocked up with casks of Madeira wine which would keep on the voyage. The ship did carry 'a machine for sweetening foul water' which consisted of a large *copper* in which sea water was boiled and the steam caught when it condensed in bottles and stored ready for use. However, such machines could not supply enough distilled water for the needs of a ship, mainly because there was not enough wood fuel available to keep this machine going as well as the stove for cooking meals. Apart from fresh water and wine Cook also took on fresh beef and onions. He was very concerned to combat scurvy and he was convinced that fresh food must be eaten whenever it was available if the wretched disease was to be prevented. Some of the men objected to the beef but to show them that he was in earnest and that he 27 would have no mutiny on his ship, Cook taught them and the whole crew a lesson. On 16 September, Able Seaman Henry Stephens and Marine Thomas Dunster were stripped to the waist and each given 12 lashes. The next day Cook issued to the whole ship's company 20 pounds of onions per man, and this time there were no objections.

The stay at Madeira lasted six days and Banks spent it collecting specimens of plants and generally observing the people and their life. He decided that 'the people here in general seem to be as idle, or rather uninformed a set as I ever yet saw' but he was impressed with the hospital which some Franciscan friars kept and particularly intrigued by a small chapel in the convent there, 'whose whole lining, *wainscote*, and ceiling, was intirely compos'd of human bones, two large thigh bones across, and a skull in each of the openings'.

Back at sea on 19 September Banks and his party turned from botany and resumed their growing interests in *marine biology*. The striking thing about Joseph Banks was his *insatiable* curiosity. Plant and tree, fish and fowl, insect, animal and man, all these Banks was prepared to study and observe with equal enthusiasm and energy. As the voyage across the Atlantic continued Banks and Solander collected all sorts of specimens. Some were preserved in spirit, some were *dissected*, some were drawn by the artists. Such activities were new to Cook but he was not the sort of man who would scorn them. It was the first chance he had had to mix with men who had studied at the universities and in the evenings no doubt he talked to them about their interests and theories as they all sipped Madeira in the large cabin. Cook got on well with people and so did Banks; both must have learned much from each other.

On 25 October the 'Endeavour' crossed the Equator and the usual ceremony of ducking all those who had never been so far south before was practised. Cook himself had never before crossed the line, but it would not have been good for discipline if he had been ducked so he excused himself, and
28 paid his *forfeit* in rum. All the others had either to be ducked

Lobster-Krill, Atlantic drawn by S. Parkinson

Galgra armata

Sydney Parkinson pinxit

Bougainvillea spectabilis, Brazil drawn by S. Parkinson

or pay a forfeit of rum or brandy. Banks and Solander chose to pay rather than take a wetting and Banks paid also for his servants and his two dogs. His Journal tells us what happened to the rest.

'Many of the Men however chose to be ducked rather than give up 4 days allowance of wine which was the price fixed upon, and as for the boys they are always ducked of course; so that about 21 underwent the ceremony which was performed thus:

'A block was made fast to the end of the main yard and a long line *reved* through it, to which three cross pieces of wood were fastnd, one of which was put between the leggs of the man who was to be duckd and to this he was tyed very fast, another was for him to hold in his hands and the third was over his head least the rope should be hoisted too near the block and by that means the man be hurt. When he was fastened upon this machine the Boatswain gave the command by his whistle and the man was hoisted up as high as the cross piece over his head would allow, when another signal was made and immediately the rope was let go and his own weight carried him down, he was then immediately hoisted up again and three times served in this manner which was every man's allowance. Thus ended the diversion of the day, for the ducking lasted till almost night. . . .'

Rio de Janeiro was reached on 13 November and Cook put in to her harbour hoping to obtain fresh water and buy fresh fruit and vegetables. Rio was a Portuguese port and as Great Britain and Portugal were allies, Cook expected friendly treatment. He did not get it. The Viceroy thought that Cook was engaged in some illegal trade and refused to believe his story that he was bound on an expedition to observe the transit of Venus. It seemed to the Viceroy to be a cock-and-bull story, invented to cover up some secret purposes. He let Cook obtain water and fresh provisions but he refused to allow the officers and Banks ashore. Eager to get specimens of plants, Banks sent his servants for them and over 200 were collected. In fact

Banks slipped ashore one morning before it was light and spent a day there before returning under the cover of dark, but it was an isolated visit. Cook took on his fresh supplies as quickly as he could, and the repair of sails and rigging and the *caulking* of the ship went forward at a good pace, but it was not until 7 December that the 'Endeavour' could slip away from that unwelcoming harbour.

Sailing south some 2,000 miles Cook reached Tierra del Fuego on 11 January 1769. Christmas Day had passed uneventfully except that all the hands got drunk. Cook's orders were to round Cape Horn rather than sail through the Straits of Magellan, so the 'Endeavour' went further south and through the Straits of Le Maire between Tierra del Fuego and Staten Island. Banks and Dr Solander went by boat to Staten Island in search of botanical specimens, and as Banks reported, 'found many plants, about 100, tho' we were not ashore above 4 hours'. On 16 January Cook anchored in the Bay of Success, off the most easterly coast of Tierra del Fuego. He wanted to make last preparations before rounding the Horn. Wood and water were taken on board, the guns were taken down into the hold and the rigging and ropes renewed where necessary. The weather was now bitterly cold and the snow lay thick on Tierra del Fuego. All the men were issued with 'a *Fearnought* jacket and a pair of *Towsers* after which,' wrote Cook, 'I never heard one man complain of cold not but the weather was cold enough.' Cook went on shore and met the 30 or so natives who came down to meet them. They were not frightened and three of them went on board the 'Endeavour'. As Cook observed they seemed to be a hardy people for they wore little but a few skins taken from *llamas* or seals and painted the rest of their body with red and black stripes. Even their houses, shaped like a beehive and made of branches and grass, gave little protection against the weather, which now grew particularly cold and snowy. Banks took his party further inland in search of plant specimens but Buchan the artist had an *epileptic* fit and the two Negro servants were frozen to death when the party had to stay a night out in the open.

Inhabitants of Tierra Del Fuego in their hut, drawn by Alexander Buchan

On 20 January the voyage round the Horn began. It took Cook 33 days but this was good going, for the passage through the Straits of Magellan had often taken three months. The doubling of Cape Horn was greatly feared for its gales and rough seas, but on this occasion Cook was lucky for they met little of the rough weather that other ships had struggled with in that area. Once past the Horn Cook sailed some 600 miles to the south-west touching 60°S., but he found no sign of land. Turning north-west he sailed steadily on until he reached the latitude 17°S. in which his destination Tahiti, or King George's Island as it was called, would be found. By 7 April he had reached this *parallel* and Cook now sailed east until on 11 April 1769 as Cook records 'at 6 am saw King Georges Island . . . it appear'd very high and mountainous'.

Captain Samuel Wallis in the 'Dolphin' had discovered Tahiti in 1767 and the Admiralty and the Royal Society had agreed that the island would be a very suitable site from which to observe the transit of Venus. This was due on 3 June so Cook had arrived in good time. Wallis had stayed on the

Tahitian Double Canoes, drawn by S. Parkinson

island some five weeks while his sick men recovered and he found the islanders very friendly. In 1768 a French expedition under Bougainville had also landed at Tahiti but had stayed only thirteen days. Cook was to be here for nearly two months at the very least, and as he neared the island he probably wondered how he and his men would get on with the Tahitians. His visit to Tahiti was not only in the service of science and astronomy but also a test in human relations, to see how *tolerant* these western sailors could be in meeting the people and ways of a different eastern civilisation.

We may imagine that Cook re-read his Admiralty Instructions as he approached his anchorage in Matavai Bay at the north of the island.

'You are to endeavour by all proper means to cultivate a friendship with the Natives, presenting them such Trifles as may be acceptable to them, exchanging with them for Provisions . . . such of the Merchandise you have been directed to Provide, as they may value, and shewing them every kind of Civility and regard. But as Captn Wallis has

33

Breadfruit, Tahiti drawn by S. Parkinson

represented the Island to be very populous, and the Natives . . . to be rather treacherous than otherwise you are to be Cautious not to let yourself be surprizéd by them, but to be constantly on your guard against any accident.'

Wallis had received at first a very friendly reception but when he had sent two of the 'Dolphin's' boats to find an anchorage they had been attacked by the Tahitians and Wallis had opened fire on them. It was only after several days of skirmishing that agreement had been reached. It was no wonder then that Cook was cautious. As the 'Endeavour' approached, swarms of canoes came out to meet her, full of excited friendly Tahitians. Lieutenants Hickes and Gore and the Master, Robert Molyneux, had been before with Wallis and they were recognised by some of the natives, and in particular by an elderly chief called Owhaa. Anchorage was safely made—it was now the 13th April 1769—and Cook and Banks went ashore. They were treated to a grand tour of some five miles through 'groves of coconut and bread fruit trees loaded with a *profusion* of fruit and giving' according to Banks 'the most grateful shade I have ever experienced'.

The next day some of the native chiefs visited the 'Endeavour' and Cook had his first sight of that petty thieving which the Tahitians seemed to specialise in. It became a constant cause of tension between the two peoples but Cook dealt with it firmly and tactfully and throughout his stay peaceful relations were preserved. Cook and some of the other gentlemen on board returned with the visitors to the land and were well feasted and entertained by two chiefs whom they decided to call Hercules and Lycurgus. Cook's Journal tells us what happened next and also shows us that the stealing which the Tahitians so much liked was done more for the fun of it than in greed for more possessions.

'Notwithstanding the care we took Dr. Solander and Dr. Monkhouse had each of them their pockets pick'd, the one his spy glass and the other of his snuff box. As soon as Lycurgus was made acquainted with the theft he dispersed the people in a moment and the method he made use of was to lay hold of the first thing that came in his way and throw it at them . . . he seemed very much concerned for what had happened and by way of recompence offered us everything that was in his house, but we refused . . . and made signs to him that we only wanted the things again. He had already sent people out after them and it was not long before they were returned . . . in the evening we returned on board very well satisfied with our little excursion.'

Cook decided not to take any chances and on 15 April work began on a fort which would serve both as a defence and as an observing point for the transit of Venus. A site was chosen on the eastern side of Matavai Bay. Work had hardly begun when one of the natives pushed down a sentry whom Cook had posted, snatched his musket and ran off with it. The midshipman in charge ordered the marines to fire and the thief was killed and other natives wounded. It was a regrettable incident. As Banks wrote 'we retired to the ship not well pleased with the days expedition, guilty no doubt in some measure of the death of a man who the most severe laws . . . would not have condemned to so severe a punishment'. It was some days before good relations were restored between the natives and the visitors.

Banks had leisure to continue his scientific observations. These now included the study of the people and their way of life as well as the plants and wildlife of the island. His party had suffered one tragic loss. Alexander Buchan, the artist, had another epileptic fit and died on 17 April. Nevertheless the collecting of specimens and the drawing of fishes and plants went on, though Banks very much regretted the death of Buchan since 'no account of the figures and dresses of men can be satisfactory unless illustrated with figures' and Sydney Parkinson was mainly a botanical draftsman, not a figure artist. The most troublesome hindrance to the work of making drawings of the various specimens was the flies. As Banks put it, 'they eat the painter's colours off the paper as fast as they can be laid on, and if a fish is to be drawn there is more trouble in keeping them off it than in the drawing itself'.

On 2 May there was another theft which greatly annoyed Cook. The *quadrant*, a heavy instrument in a packing case eighteen inches square, was stolen. Moreover, it was taken out of the newly finished fort which had an earth bank of $4\frac{1}{2}$ feet on its inside and a ditch 10 feet broad and 6 feet deep on the outside, with 2 four pounders and 6 swivels for its defence and sentries on constant duty. It was eventually recovered after 36 Cook had sent out an armed search party.

House and Plantations of Tahitian Chief, drawn by S. Parkinson

Men's Dress, Tahiti

At last June 3rd came and Cook made his observations of the transit at Fort Venus, for so he had named his fort. Green also made observations from another point and all seemed to have gone well. In fact, however, it proved impossible to calculate the sun's distance from the readings.

Cook had now finished the first part of his orders for the expedition: he had found Tahiti and he had observed the transit of Venus. His Instructions from the Admiralty also suggested that if he had the opportunity, he should also

'make such farther surveys and plans, and take such views of the Island, its harbours and bays, as you conceive may be useful to Navigation or necessary to give us a more perfect idea and description than we have hitherto received of it.'

Cook did find time for this towards the end of June while his men worked on the 'Endeavour'. The sides of the ship had to be *careened* and then coated with pitch and brimstone. The bottom of the 'Endeavour' was found to be free of worm but the longboat needed major repairs, for her bottom 'was like a honeycomb and some of the holes $\frac{1}{8}$ of an inch in diameter, such a progress has this destructive insect made in six weeks'. There were various other repairs needed and fresh provisions had also to be stowed aboard. While his men finished off these jobs Cook and Banks set off in the pinnace with a native as guide, and made a full circuit of the island. They took four days over it and arrived back at the fort on 1 July having made a plan of the island with Cook's usual thoroughness and accuracy.

Cook was now eager to leave Tahiti. Their stay had been an interesting and a successful one. They had made good friends of the Tahitians, and the island would now be a future port of call for British ships in the Pacific. They had also learned much of Tahitian ways of life. Among these, two were the most interesting. First they had been introduced to roast dog—a special Tahitian dog—as a dish for dinner. 'Queen' Obarea, a female chieftain of some charm, was always visiting the 'Endeavour' and one day she brought the officers a dog as a

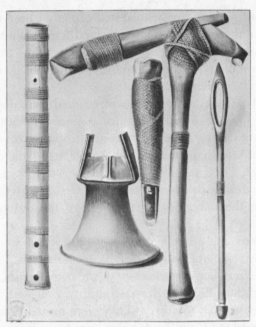

Tahitian tools: flute, stone pestle used to pulp their food, small axe, chisel of human bone, thatching needle

gift. Cook's Journal tells us how it was dressed and cooked. 'They [the natives] first made a hole in the ground about a foot deep in which they made a fire and heated some small stones. While this was doing the dog was strangled and the hair got off by laying him frequently upon the fire, and as clean as if it had been scalded off with hot water, his *entrails* were taken out and the whole washed clean, and as soon as the stones and hole was sufficiently heated, the fire was put out, and part of the stones were left in the bottom of the hole, upon these stones were laid green leaves and upon them the dog together with the entrails. These were likewise covered with leaves and over them hot stones, and then the whole was close covered with mould. After it had laid here about 4 hours, the Oven was opened and the dog taken out whole and well done, and it was the 39 opinion of every one who tasted of it that they never eat sweeter meat, we therefore resolved for the future not to despise dogs' flesh. It is in this manner that the natives dress, or bake all their victuals that require it, flesh, fish and fruit.'

Secondly, Cook and his crew discovered tattooing. At the age of 13 or 14 the young Tahitians underwent the painful operation of having their buttocks and stomachs covered with designs cut into their skin by a sharp piece of bone dipped in a black dye. They were very proud of their tattoos and several of the 'Endeavour's' crew, including Cook, had their arms marked in this way. So the tradition of the tattooed sailor began.

There was one other feature of Tahiti which Cook's crew would long remember, the attractive friendly girls. Just before the 'Endeavour' was due to sail on 9 July two marines, Clement Webb and Sam Gibson, deserted and ran off with two girls whom they wanted to marry. They were brought back under armed guard and confined below until 14 July when the 'Endeavour' was then at sea and any more thought of desertion was impossible. The two marines were given two dozen lashes each as a punishment and so the affair ended, except for memories.

The air was filled with the noise of men and women crying as the 'Endeavour' set sail on 13 July 1769. Cook had allowed only two of the Tahitians to come with them, though many had begged for a place. These were Tupia, a chief and a priest, and his servant Taiata. As they sailed away Banks and Tupia climbed to the masthead and waved to the canoes. There is no record of Cook's actions at this time but we may imagine that he went to his cabin to read the secret additional instructions which the Admiralty had given him. For at the end of the Instructions which told him to observe the transit of Venus and survey King George's Island, were these words.

'When this Service is perform'd, you are to put to Sea without Loss of Time, and carry into execution the Additional Instructions contained in the inclosed Sealed Packet.'

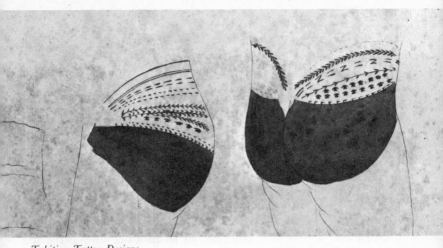

Tahitian Tattoo Designs

Tahitian Dancing, by J. Webber

6   New Zealand

These additional instructions show quite clearly what the main motive of the Government was in supporting the Royal Society's expedition. For they order Cook to sail south to a latitude of 40° and discover the Southern Continent, making maps and charts of it, and noting its produce and gathering specimens of its minerals, trees and fruits. Cook is also ordered to 'endeavour by all proper means to cultivate a friendship and alliance' with the natives.

> 'You are also with the Consent of the Natives to take possession of Convenient Situations in the Country in the Name of the King of Great Britain; or, if you find the Country uninhabited take Possession for his Majesty by setting up Proper Marks and Inscriptions, as first discoverers and possessors.'

In order to avoid the worst of the winter which rages at that time in the southern latitudes, Cook spent a month exploring the group of islands to the north-west of Tahiti, which he called the Society Islands because, as Cook put it, 'they lay *contiguous* to one another'. People have since thought that he named them after the Royal Society, but it was not so. The Journals of both Cook and Banks are full of interesting descriptions of the life of the natives of these islands and they obviously spent a happy time exploring them, but by 15 August Cook was determined to be off on his mission and wrote that he 'was now fully resolved to stand directly to the Southward in search of the Continent'.

He sailed south for a fortnight until he reached 40°S, but 42 no sign of land was seen. The sea was heavy with a large swell

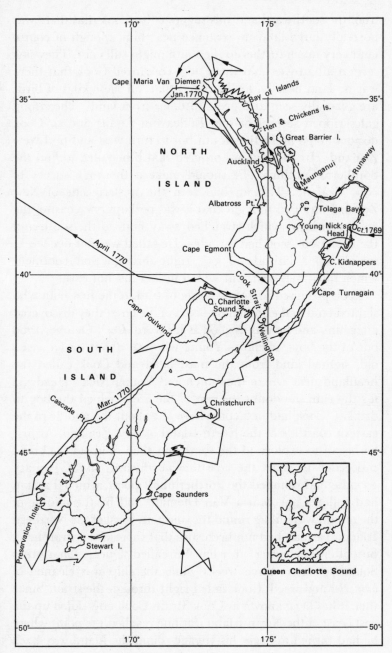

Cook's Circumnavigation of New Zealand

43

from the southward and this suggested to Cook that there was no really large land in existence near him, though of course land very much further to the south might still exist. They saw several albatrosses and these, too, convinced Cook that there was no land nearby, for he noted that 'all these kind of birds are generally seen at a great distance from land'. The strong gales ripped several of the 'Endeavour's' sails and so Cook decided to go no further south but to turn west and find New Zealand. His Instructions ordered that if he failed to find the Southern Continent, he should make a thorough survey of New Zealand. Tasman had seen the western side of New Zealand and had thought that it was perhaps one coast of the great continent which stretched away both to the south and the east. Cook scotched this idea. He sailed west for five weeks mainly on a latitude of 35°, right through that continent which men imagined, but which in fact did not exist.

Cook promised to give a bottle of rum to the first man who sighted land and also to name part of the coast they discovered after him, and he was as good as his word. On 7 October 1769 one of the boys, Nicholas Young who was about twelve years old, sighted land from the mast head and Cook called the headland near where they anchored Young Nick's Head. As for the rum, no doubt the rest of the crew helped the boy to drink it. Cook had in fact anchored at about the middle of the eastern coastline of the North Island of New Zealand. At first he began to explore to the south but then doubled back and proceeded to chart the coastline northwards. By 1 January 1770 he had rounded the northernmost point, which Tasman had called Cape Maria Van Dieman, and by the middle of the month was sailing round the southern coast of the Northern Island. Tasman had not been sure that there was a strait here, but after anchoring in what he called Queen Charlotte's Sound for some three weeks while the ship was cleaned of *barnacles* and weed, Cook sailed right through the strait. Since then it has been known as Cook Strait. Cook now sailed up the east coast of the North Island until he reached the point where he had turned to begin his voyage round the island way back in October 1769. By doing this he proved that the land was indeed an island. Cook had called the headland there Cape Turnagain, for the obvious reason, and once again it was to be a turning point, for Cook now turned south and began his voyage to see if the Southern Continent lay in that direction.

He sailed as close as he could to the east coast of the South Island, and he charted its main features, though he was not always close enough to chart all the inlets. Even when rounding its southernmost point he was not able to see the strait between Stewart Island and the mainland and he recorded it as a *peninsula*. Then sailing northwards he quickly charted the western coast and arrived back in Cook Strait on 27 March 1770. He had proved that New Zealand consisted of two islands, and he had shown that, if 'Terra Australis Incognita' did exist, New Zealand was not part of it. His survey was not as detailed as those he had, for example, completed in Newfoundland, but nevertheless it was the first time that any explorer had made such a detailed study of so large an unknown land. Cook's Journal is full of information, not only of the coastline, but also of the landscape and the people of New Zealand.

The natives of New Zealand, the Maoris, were not so friendly as the Tahitians had been. They had a similar language and Tupia was able to converse with them, but they were more aggressive and threw stones at the sailors. They were not easily frightened. Even gunshot fired over their heads did not always make them run away. When Cook first met the natives in October 1769, there was a skirmish in which four Maoris were killed. Cook was very upset about it, but he felt that he had to shoot to kill rather than 'suffer either my self or those that were with me to be knocked on the head'. After that, relations with the natives varied. Some were very friendly as at Tolaga Bay where Cook was able to trade with them and secure fresh water and vegetables. Others were hostile. For example the day after leaving Tolaga Bay on 30 October 1769, Cook made this entry in his Journal.

'At 9 five canoes came off to us, in one of which were

Watering Place, Tolaga Bay a sketch by Cook himself

upwards of 40 men all armed with *pikes* &c. From this and other circumstances it fully appeared that they came with no friendly intention, and . . . . I ordered a *grapeshot* to be fired a little wide of them. This made them pull off a little and then they got together either to consult what to do or to look about them, upon this I ordered a round shot to be fired over their heads which frightened them to that degree that I believe they did not think themselves safe until they got ashore; this occasioned our calling the point of land off which this happened Cape Runaway.'

After this there were no major skirmishes with the Maoris and some made Cook particularly welcome. At the Bay of Islands on 4 December the natives showed Cook round their fortified village and traded him fish for 'meer trifles' as pieces of cloth and paper. At Queen Charlotte's Sound, where they had quite a long stay, Cook found convincing evidence, however, that he must always be wary of the Maoris. For though they were friendly enough to Cook, he discovered that they could deal with those they took a dislike to, quickly and savagely. Cook's entry in his Journal on 17 January 1770 makes this clear.

Fortified Village, Bay of Islands by S. Parkinson

'Some of us went in the Pinnace into another cove not far from where the ship lays; in going thither we met with a woman floating upon the water who to all appearance had not been dead many days. Soon after we landed we met with two or three of the natives who not long before must have been regailing themselves upon human flesh, for I got from one of them the bone of the forearm of a man or a woman which was quite fresh and the flesh had been lately picked off which they told us they had eat. They gave us to understand that but a few days ago they had taken killed and eat a boat's crew of their enemies or strangers, for I believe that they look upon all strangers as enemies; from what we could learn the Woman we had seen floating upon the water was in this boat and had been drowned in the fray. There was not one of us that had the least doubt but what this people were canabals but the finding this bone with part of the sinews fresh upon it was a stronger proof than any we had yet met with, and in order to be fully satisfied of the truth of what they had told us, we told one of them that it was not the bone of a man but that of a dog, but he with great fervency took hold of his 47

Maori War canoe, by S. Parkinson

forearm and told us again that it was that bone and to
convince us that they had eat the flesh he took hold of the
flesh of his own arm with his teeth and made shew of
eating.'

The Journal of Joseph Banks also provides us with detailed
descriptions of New Zealand and its inhabitants: the language
of the people, how they ate and dressed, how they made their
weapons, their canoes and their houses. He also describes as
we might expect, the natural life of the islands. He notes the
various species of birds and fish and observes, quite rightly in
fact, that there were no four-footed animals or quadrupeds
native to New Zealand. Dogs and rats there were but these
had probably migrated there. As a botanist, Banks was dis-
appointed with the lack of variety in the plant life he found,
but on the other hand he was delighted that most of the specimens they found had never been described by botanists before.

'The intire novelty however of the greatest part of what
we found recompens'd us as natural historians for the want

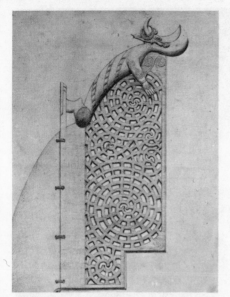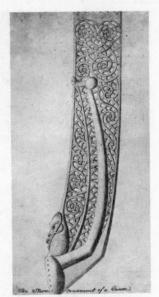

Head and Stern of a New Zealand canoe

of variety. Sow thistle, garden nightshade, and perhaps
1 or 2 kinds of Grasses were exactly the same as in England,
3 or 4 kinds of Fern the same as those of the West Indies,
and a plant or 2 that are common to almost all the world:
these were all that had before been described by any
botanist out of 400 species, except 5 or 6 which we our-
selves had before seen in Terra del Fuego.'

By his exploration of New Zealand Cook had now completed
his Instructions. He wanted to return home by way of Cape
Horn so that he could prove the existence or non-existence of
the Southern Continent, which still remained in doubt, but
after consulting with his officers and noting that it would mean
sailing through 'the very depth of winter' in those southern
latitudes, he decided to come home via the Cape of Good
Hope. The 'Endeavour' needed various repairs, too, so one
advantage of the latter route would be that they could call in
at Batavia and refit and take on supplies as necessary. There
was another advantage in this route. It offered Cook the   49

Portrait of a New Zealand Man

chance of finding and exploring the east coast of what was then known as New Holland, but which we know as Australia. Cook was not the man to refuse such an opportunity and on 1 April 1770 they left the coast of New Zealand and steered north-west for New Holland.

7 Australia

The Dutch had mapped the western coast of New Holland in the first half of the seventeenth century. They had also recorded nearly half of its southern coast and Tasman had discovered what is now called Tasmania, though he had not found out whether it was part of New Holland or a separate land. In the north the Dutch had mapped the New Holland coastline as far as and including the Gulf of Carpentaria, but the eastern coast was still unknown. Also it was still not known for certain that Torres Strait existed and many imagined that New Holland joined New Guinea. So when Cook left New Zealand on 1 April 1770 he knew he was on the track of great geographical discoveries and the answers to questions which had puzzled men for centuries.

Cook hoped first to sight Van Diemen's Land, or Tasmania as it is now called, and settle the question of whether or not it was part of New Holland. However, gales forced him northwards and Cook missed Van Diemen's Land. It was not until 1798 that the explorer Matthew Flinders proved that Van Diemen's Land was an island. Incidentally it was this same Matthew Flinders who suggested the name Australia for New Holland and this name was officially agreed in 1817. To avoid confusion it will be best to call this land that Cook was now nearing by its official name of Australia and not by the name of New Holland which its first discoverers, the Dutch, had given it. Moreover, it must be remembered that Australia was not the 'Terra Australis Incognita', or the unknown southern continent, despite the similarity of its name. Cook was about to explore Australia and bring back maps of its coastline, but

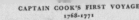

74 Banksia serrata.
from 200
Botany Bay 1770 1900

New South Wales Botany Bay. N.S.

Banksia serrata Lin. suppl.

Botany Bay

NEW HOLLAND
BANKS & SOLANDER

Isostylis serrata Britten

Illustr. Bot. Cook's Voyage, tab. 270 p. 65

it was still possible as many people believed that there was another southern continent perhaps larger than Australia somewhere to the south-east. Cook had not yet settled the question of the existence of 'Terra Australis Incognita'.

After sixteen days at sea Cook sighted a gannet and this told them that they were not far from land. Two days later the land was sighted and Cook decided to follow the coast northwards. They were in need of fresh water and Cook looked for a suitable harbour, but it was a week before he found one. On 29 April 1770 Cook anchored in what he later called Botany Bay, because of 'the great quantity of new plants &c Mr Banks & Dr Solander collected in this place'.

When Cook approached the shore the natives they had seen and hoped to meet, all made off out of sight except two who tried to oppose their landing. Even when Cook peppered them with small musket shot they refused to withdraw. One of them took up a shield and advanced against the landing party, throwing darts at them. Cook fired his musket again and this time they retired and Cook was able to approach their huts. All the adults had gone away leaving only children there and Cook gave them some beads. There was no sign of fresh water so Cook returned to his boats again and went to the north side of the bay. Here they found water, enough to provision the ship, but once again they failed to make friends with the natives, for they backed away the moment Cook or any of his party approached. In fact the Australian *aborigines* were quite unlike the friendly Tahitians and although Cook stayed in Botany Bay until 6 May, the natives refused to come near them.

Banks and Solander found themselves in a botanist's paradise. One notable find was the plant *Banksia* and by the time they left the bay they had a vast collection of specimens, so much so that storing them was a great problem. Nevertheless their finds led to the naming of a Bay which was to become famous in both British and Australian history, for in 1788 the British sent their convict settlers to Australia and they landed in Botany Bay.

Banksia serrata. Red Honeysuckle, Botany Bay

Cook continued slowly northward up the coast and did not anchor again until on 23 May they reached Bustard Bay, so called because the crew feasted themselves on the ducks and *bustards* they found there in abundance. They did not stay long for Cook was not altogether happy about the way his crew was behaving and he wanted to press on with the voyage. There had been an unpleasant incident when one of the men, Orton the clerk, had had his clothes and parts of his ears cut off as he lay in a drunken sleep one night. Cook never found the culprit, and the matter worried him. He wrote, 'I look upon such proceedings as highly dangerous in such voyages as this and the greatest insult that could be offer'd to my authority in this ship, as I have always been ready to hear and *redress* every complaint that have been made against any Person in the Ship.'

As Cook continued northwards navigation became more difficult. The coast abounded in shoals and the ship's boats were very busy sounding out a passage for the 'Endeavour'. Unperturbed Cook went on steadily, charting the inlets and islands and naming them with the names of the British aristocracy as Rockingham Bay, Cape Sandwich and Fitzroy Island. Unbeknown to Cook, however, there lurked another danger. He was sailing between the coast and the Great Barrier Reef which at its southern end is almost two hundred miles from the coast but which draws nearer the coast as it runs north westwards. This mountain of coral rises from the depths of the ocean and spreading out towards the shore makes the coastal waters a mass of barriers. In spite of the difficulties Cook went on. He was not the sort of man who would turn back when there were questions such as the existence of Torres Strait to be answered.

Cook kept his leadsmen out continually sounding the depths of the water and up aloft he had lookouts. On 11 June in the evening the leadsman suddenly found the depth of water decreasing, from 21 to 12, and then to 10 and 8 *fathom*. It then increased to 17 fathom and all seemed well when the 'Endeavour' stuck on the coral. It says much for the leadership of

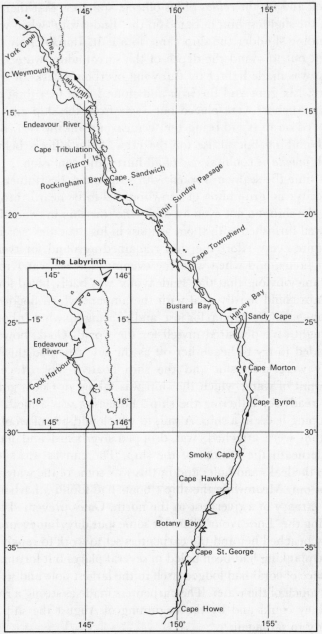

Cook's navigation of the east coast of Australia

55

Cook and for the *calibre* of his officers and crew that there was not the slightest hint of panic on the 'Endeavour' when with a grinding shudder the ship came to a halt. Immediately boats went out to sound the depth of the surrounding waters. The ship was made lighter by throwing overboard casks of water, stores, six guns and the iron and stone *ballast* to a total of 50 tons. Anchors were placed out away from the ship and then heaved on to try to bring the 'Endeavour' off the reef. Banks had nothing but praise for the crew. 'The officers behaved with *inimitable* coolness *void* of all hurry and confusion. . . . All this time the seamen worked with surprising cheerfulness and alacrity; no grumbling or growling was to be heard throughout the ship, no not even an oath (tho' the ship in general was as well furnished with them as most in his majesties' service).' Despite every effort the ship remained aground for twenty-four hours, and when with the evening tide the water rose it became obvious that the 'Endeavour' was badly holed for the pumps could hardly deal with the amount which flooded in. Banks gave the ship up for lost 'and packing up what I thought I might save prepared myself for the worst'. Cook, however, decided to try to heave her off as the tide rose and this time they were successful and the ship floated. To reduce the amount of water which the ship was taking in Cook 'got the sail ready for fothering the ship'. Fothering was a method of stopping leaks in a ship. A sail, to which odd bits of wool and oakum were attached, was dropped overboard and hauled underneath the bottom of the ship. The canvas was sucked into the leaks and holes and in this way some of the water was kept out. Meanwhile the ship's boats had found a harbour in the estuary of a river just to the north. Gales prevented them taking the 'Endeavour' there for some four days but eventually they beached her and the carpenters set to work to repair her. The planking had been holed in several places but fortunately a piece of coral had lodged itself in the largest hole and so kept out much of the water. The carpenters made as strong a repair as they could and by the beginning of August the ship was

56   ready to sail again.

The delay had had some good results. Banks and Solander increased their store of botanical specimens and also, with great delight, studied the varied fish, animal and bird life. Most notable of all, they discovered the kangaroo, and found that it 'proved excellent meat'. They also managed to meet some of the Australian aborigines and in their Journals Cook and Banks have left us the first *authentic* account that we have of these natives. They were in general about 5 feet 6 inch in height, slender but nimble and very active. They wore no clothes and their skin was, according to Banks, the colour of chocolate, 'not that their skins were so dark but the smoke and dirt with which they were all cased over . . . made them of that colour'. Their hair was cropped close to their heads but 'of the same *consistence* with our hair, by no means wooly or curld like that of Negroes'. They painted some parts of their bodies with red and white paint, either in lines or in large patches. Cook found their voices 'soft and tunable' though neither he nor Tupia could understand their language. Their most notable feature was their nose as Cook records in his Journal.

'One of these men had a hole through the bridge of his nose in which he stuck a piece of bone as thick as my finger, seeing this we examined all their noses and found that they had all holes for the same purpose, they had likewise holes in their ears but no ornaments hanging to them, they had bracelets upon their arms made of hair and like hoops of small cord; they sometimes must wear a kind of *fillet* about their heads for one of them applied some part of an old shirt I had given them to this use.'

However, relations with these natives were little better than they had been with those in Botany Bay. One day the sailors caught a huge turtle on the reef and some of the natives came on board expecting part of it. When they were refused they tried to throw overboard all that they could lay their hands on and when they were frightened back to the land they set fire to the bush around the camp that the crew had made. Fortunately most of the stores and all the gunpowder had by that time been reloaded back into the ship, for the fire spread

rapidly. As Banks wrote, 'this accident will however be a sufficient warning for us if ever we should again pitch tents in such a climate to burn everything round us before we begin'. Just before they left Banks went 'botanizing' and found a pile of the clothes which they had given the natives as presents, 'left all in a heap together, doubtless as lumber not worth carriage'. It made Banks reflect on the difference between these people 'content with little nay almost nothing, [and] far enough removed from the anxieties attending upon riches' and the Europeans who constantly search for more wealth and luxuries. Since then many people have imagined that if only they could get away from civilisation and back to nature life would be perfect and happy, but it does not seem to be as simple as that. Certainly there was not one man on the 'Endeavour', who would have stayed behind. After almost two years at sea they longed for home and the comforts of western civilisation.

On 6 August Cook left the safety of the river he had, quite naturally, named Endeavour River. He decided to make for Torres Strait hoping that it existed and that it would bring them quickly to a dockyard in Batavia. Outside the river, sailing once again was full of difficulty and danger so Cook decided to go east and sail outside the area of the reef. However, he found the open sea worse for its great breakers threatened to carry the ship crashing onto the reef. Cook looked for an opening and managed to pass back again into the waters between the land and the reef, 'happy once more to encounter those shoals which but two days ago our utmost wishes were crowned by getting clear of'. He continued to the northernmost point of the coast and named it York Cape 'in honour of His late Royal Highness the Duke of York'. Though he knew that he could make no claim to having discovered Australia, he was confident that no European had ever explored its eastern coast before, so he landed and hoisted the English flag and 'in the name of His Majesty King George the Third took possession of the whole eastern coast'.

Cook now proved to the world that Torres had found a 59

strait between New Guinea and Australia. He sailed through it and then westwards on first to Savu for fresh *victuals* and then to Batavia for that refit which the 'Endeavour' now badly needed. He anchored there on 10 October 1770. It took more than two months to repair the ship and it was not until 26 December that they could leave for the final leg of their journey round the Cape of Good Hope. Their long stay in Batavia had been fateful. It was a place notorious for disease and illness. Malaria and dysentery struck Cook's crew. Seven men died while they were there, including Monkhouse, the surgeon, and Tupia, the Tahitian. When they sailed Cook noted that 'The number sick on board at this time amounts to 40 or upwards and the rest of the Ship's company are in a weakly condition, having been every one sick except the sailmaker an old man about 70 or 80 years of age, and what was still more extraordinary in this man his being generally more or less drunk every day.' However, not even drink could preserve the old sailmaker for the 'Endeavour' carried disease with her and on 27 January 1771, John Ravenhill, Sailmaker, died. Sydney Parkinson, the artist died the same day and Charles Green, the astronomer, two days later. Altogether thirty men died between leaving Batavia and reaching England, including lieutenant Hickes and Molyneux the master. Cook called at the Cape and at St Helena and eventually anchored in the Downs on 13 July 1771.

It had been a momentous voyage. The coastline of New Zealand had been circumnavigated, the eastern coast of Australia had been explored, and the existence of Torres Strait had been proved. A vast amount of scientific material had been gathered. There were the observations of the transit of Venus and notes about the behaviour of the compass and about tides. There was the huge natural history collection of Banks and Solander. There were boxes of articles taken from the various peoples they had met, which would illustrate the different life of the natives of the Pacific. The Royal Society, the Admiralty and the general public were all interested to learn more and the Admiralty engaged a certain Dr John

61

Cook's First Voyage in H.M.S. 'Endeavour' 1768–1771

Hawkesworth to write up a lengthy account of the voyage based on the journals of Cook and Banks.

Strangely enough, nobody took much notice of Cook. Banks and Solander were regarded as the real heroes. Eventually Cook was presented to His Majesty at St James's Palace in August 1771. He was also promoted to commander, though this was a small increase in rank and certainly not the rank of captain he might have been given. There was no glory at the

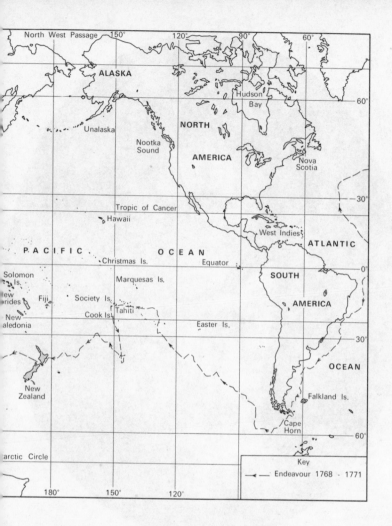

time for Cook, but he was not the sort of character who would worry about such things. He had the satisfaction of knowing that he had done an extremely difficult task well. His crew knew this too and so do we who can see it with the hindsight that history gives us.

Cook retired to his home at Mile End and his family. Two of his children, Elizabeth and Joseph had died in his absence, but his two other boys Nathaniel and James then about eight 63

Engraving after portrait of James Cook by G. Webber

and seven years old no doubt gave him all the hero-worship
he wanted. He settled down to his papers and his charts and
also his plans. Australia had been explored but the question
of the existence of another southern continent still remained
and both the Admiralty and Cook wanted to settle it.

8   The Second Voyage, 1772–1775

Both British and French statesmen were still eager to find out whether there was land in the South Seas which they could turn to the profit of their countries. In 1739 the Frenchman Bouvet had sighted what he took to be continental land in the South Atlantic, calling it Cape Circumcision. It turned out to be an island (Bouvet Island) but his report was a great spur to the French and while Cook had been away they had launched several expeditions. If there was a continent the British wanted to discover it first and only five weeks after his return the Admiralty asked Cook to prepare for another voyage.

Two Whitby colliers were bought, the 'Drake' 462 tons and the 'Raleigh' 340 tons. However, to avoid offending the Spanish who had cause to remember such famous names the ships were soon renamed the 'Resolution' and 'Adventure'. Joseph Banks wanted to go on this voyage, too, and he persuaded Lord Sandwich, the First Lord of the Admiralty, to order alterations to be made to the 'Resolution' so that she would be more comfortable for his party. Cook was against this but rather than make trouble he said nothing. The ship was given an upper deck and other alterations but when the time came to sail her down the Thames, she was found to be too top-heavy for safety and the alterations were removed. Banks was furious and, failing to get his own way, he withdrew from the expedition. He was annoyed with Cook but this soon passed, for neither men were the sort who enjoyed having enemies, and they remained good friends.

The main aim of the voyage was geographical discovery but

'Resolution' (model) Whitby Museum

there were also two other objects in mind. Firstly, the Admiralty wanted to test some chronometers or clocks to see if they would keep Greenwich time accurately while at sea. For if such a clock could be proved accurate it would mean that the longitude of any position could be calculated quite easily. A carpenter, John Harrison, had invented a clock which he claimed would keep accurate time and the 'Resolution' carried one of these while the 'Adventure' carried two chronometers made by John Arnold. Secondly, Cook wanted to show that

Captain Tobias Furneaux, by James Northcote

scurvy was an avoidable disease and so he had aboard various anti-scorbutic (that is, anti-scurvy) remedies. With these and his own high standards of cleanliness which he was determined as always to enforce, he hoped to avoid scurvy.

Cook left Plymouth on 13 July 1772, himself in the 'Resolution' and Captain Tobias Furneaux in command of the 'Adventure'. The plan was to explore the extreme south in the summer and retire north for the winters. They stopped for supplies at Madeira and reached Cape Town by the end of 67

October. On 23 November Cook set sail southwards in search of Bouvet's Cape Circumcision. He did not find it but he searched the area around the position given by Bouvet and so made it clear that whatever Bouvet had sighted it was not continental land but probably an island. Cook then sailed eastwards and crossed the Antarctic Circle in the middle of January 1773. It was the first time that men had sailed so far south. No one could pretend that it was easy. Icebergs and pack-ice, high winds and heavy seas were all that the crews saw for three months. The decks and rigging were covered with ice and for the sailors who had to struggle with the sails it meant frost-bitten hands and torn flesh. However, the crews remained in fairly good spirits and at least on the 'Resolution' there was no scurvy. Fresh water was obtained by melting lumps of ice and with Cook insisting on personal cleanliness, the constant changing to dry clothes, the fumigation, scrubbing and ventilation of quarters, and the use of stoves to dry out the damp, scurvy was avoided. There were, however, some complaints, particularly from the naturalist John Forster who sailed on the 'Resolution'. But he had been complaining ever since the voyage began. In the first few days he had been dissatisfied with his cabin and on failing to have it changed, he had shouted that he would report the matter to the King. After that 'I'll tell King George' had become the ships' joke and also no doubt a safety valve which would turn bad tempers into laughter when those terrible Antarctic conditions began to get men down.

In February the two ships were parted but a rendezvous had been arranged in Queen Charlotte's Sound, New Zealand. Furneaux had some cases of scurvy aboard and after touching Tasmania he arrived in the Sound in early April. Cook stayed some five weeks longer in the south and after an equally long stay at Dusky Sound on the southern coast of New Zealand, he finally rejoined the 'Adventure' on 18 May 1773. Furneaux was ready to winter in the Sound, but Cook had other plans. For example, Cook had thought of visiting Tasmania to see if it was part of Australia. Furneaux's report that this was the

The ships watering by taking in ice, 61 S. by William Hodges Jan. 1773

case made Cook give up these thoughts, though in fact Furneaux was mistaken. Instead Cook decided to sail eastwards to see if there was continental land there. None was found but the unfortunate crew of the 'Adventure' were once more smitten with scurvy, so the two ships turned northwards for Tahiti and arrived there in the middle of August.

Cook was given a friendly welcome and they had a long and pleasant stay here before sailing westwards to the Society Islands and more friendly welcomes. Here Furneaux took on board the young native man Omai and he eventually sailed with him all the way back to England. Still sailing westwards Cook reached the Friendly Islands (which include Tonga) in October and then south once more to refit at Queen Charlotte's Sound. During the voyage down the coast of the North Island of New Zealand, the 'Adventure' was driven in a storm far to the east. Cook waited for her at the Sound for three weeks but then, rather than lose his chance to explore the south during the milder season, Cook decided to sail. He left a message for Furneaux in a bottle buried near a tree and began this next stage of his voyage on 25 November 1773. The 'Adventure' arrived a few days later but Furneaux decided not to follow Cook. After a refit—during which time he lost a boat's crew of ten, killed and eaten by the Maoris—he sailed across the south seas past Cape Horn and touching at the Cape of Good Hope before reaching England on 14 July 1774.

Meanwhile Cook had achieved one of his ambitions. He does not tell us much about himself in his Journals but in the following extract dated 30 January 1774 he reveals a little. He had reached 71°S and found his way blocked by ice. 'I whose Ambition leads me not only farther than any other man has been before me, but as far as I think it possible for man to go, was not sorry at meeting with this interruption, as it in some measure relieved us from the dangers and hardships, inseparable with the Navigation of the Southern Polar Regions.'

Cook turned northwards to search for continental land in that portion of the South Pacific which so far on this voyage

Portrait of Omai, by Nathaniel Dance

he had not explored. Towards the end of February Cook was taken ill with stomach trouble. To strengthen him, Mr Forster's dog, the only live animal left on board, was killed and Cook drank the soup made from its flesh. Soon after this, whether as a result of the soup or not we shall never know, Cook recovered. The long voyage continued without sight of land until 11 March when they reached Easter Island. An exploring party landed and were as interested and mystified by the great stone statues of that island as men have been ever since. After a week here Cook set sail for the Marquesas which the Spaniards had discovered in 1595, and then on to Tahiti where he arrived on 22 April 1774.

Monuments of Easter Island, by William Hoddes

Leaving Tahiti in the middle of May Cook sailed west hoping to find the land the Portuguese Quiros had suggested was a continent in 1606. Cook did find it and explored it, showing it to be a collection of islands which he called the New Hebrides. A little further south he discovered a new island which he named New Caledonia and then once more made for Queen Charlotte's Sound. He arrived here towards the end of October and heard from the natives news of the 'Adventure', though naturally enough he did not get the true story of the loss of her boat's crew.

On 11 November 1774 Cook began the voyage home. Across the South Pacific he reached Cape Horn on 21 Decem- 73

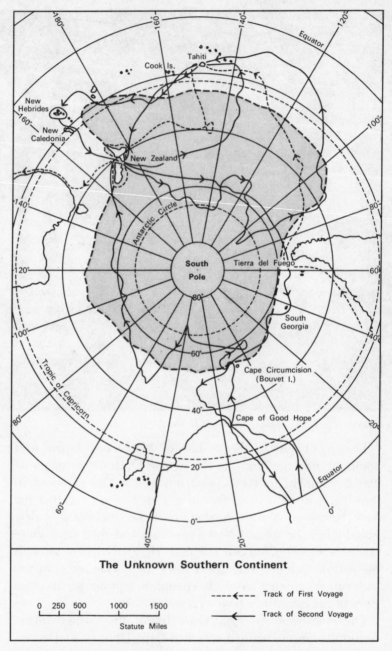

The Unknown Southern Continent

----◄----	Track of First Voyage
——◄——	Track of Second Voyage

0 250 500 1000 1500
Statute Miles

74

Map of Cook's Second Voyage, showing Terra Australis Incognita as imagined in the 18th century, superimposed by track of Cook's voyage

ber and stayed for a fortnight to explore Tierra Del Fuego before sailing across the Atlantic. He rediscovered and re-named South Georgia and sailed through the South Sandwich Islands. Once again he failed to find Bouvet's Island and crossing his outward track of 1772 he turned north and reached the Cape of Good Hope on 21 March 1775. On 30th July the 'Resolution' anchored at Portsmouth.

His great voyage received little *acclaim* in the newspapers of the day but the Admiralty were well pleased with Cook. Three important questions had been answered. First the accuracy of the Harrison chronometer, though not that of the Arnold one, had been proved. Second, Cook had shown that scurvy could be avoided. Not one man had died from that disease on the 'Resolution'. Third, Cook had shown that 'Terra Australis Incognita' did not exist. The map on page 74 shows how the tracks of Cook's voyage had sailed right over the continent which men had imagined. There was, it is true, land in the Antarctic, and Cook himself suspected this, but it was a land of ice and certainly not the land rich in *minerals* and produce, of which men had dreamed. No longer need British statesmen fear that the French or the Spanish might find a prosperous empire in the South Seas. Finally in addition to all this, Cook's Journal and the drawings of William Hodges, the artist on the voyage, brought back more knowledge of life in the islands of the Pacific.

Cook once again met the King at St James's Palace and talked about his voyage. He was promoted to post-captain and given a well-paid position at Greenwich Hospital. The Royal Society made him a Fellow and presented him with the Copley Gold Medal in recognition of his work to overcome scurvy. These were just rewards for Cook's exertions, and he was well satisfied. He received, too, a song written by one of his sailors, Thomas Perry. He valued this especially and it proves to us that Cook's men liked their captain. Apart from his other achievements, it was no small thing to have taken men into the extremities of the Antarctic without losing their respect for him both as a captain and a man.

THE ANTARCTIC MUSE

(A Song by Thomas Perry)

It is now my brave boys we are clear of the Sea
And keep a good heart if you'll take my advice
We are out of the cold my brave Boys do not fear
For the Cape of good Hope with good hearts we do steer

Thank God we have ranged the Globe all around
And we have likewise the south Continent found
But it being too late in the year as they say
We could stay there no longer the land to survey

So we leave it alone for we give a good reason
For the next ship that comes to survey in right season
The great fields of Ice among them we were bothered
We were forced to alter our course to the Northward

So we have done out utmost as any men born
To discover a land so far South of Cape Horn
So now my brave Boys we no longer will stay
For we leave it alone for the next Ship to survey

It was when we got into the cold frosty air
We was obliged our Mittens and Magdalen Caps to wear
We are out of the cold my brave Boys and perhaps
We will pull off our Mittens and Magdalen Caps

We are hearty and well and of good constitution
And have ranged the Globe round in the brave Resolution
Brave Captain Cook he was our Commander
Has conducted the Ship from all eminent danger

We were all hearty seamen no cold did we fear
And we have from all sickness entirely kept clear
Thanks be to the Captain he has proved so good
Amongst all the Islands to give us fresh food

And when to old England my Brave Boys we arrive
We will tip off a Bottle to make us alive
We will toast Captain Cook with a loud song all round
Because that he has the South Continent found

Blessed be to his wife and his Family too
God prosper them all and well for to do
Bless'd be unto them so long as they shall live
And that is the wish to them I do give.

9 The Third Voyage, 1776–1780

Cook was not completely happy in his comfortable and easy job at Greenwich Hospital. He wrote to his friend John Walker:

'A few Months ago the whole Southern hemisphere was hardly big enough for me and now I am going to be confined within the limits of Greenwich Hospital, which are far too small for an active mind like mine, I must however confess it is a fine retreat and a pretty income, but whether I can bring my self to like ease and retirement, time will shew.'

As it happened Cook was not in retirement for long. The Admiralty wanted to solve the question of the existence or not of a North-West Passage from the Hudson Bay round the north of America to the north Pacific. They asked Cook for his advice and he volunteered to command an expedition.

Once again there were two ships, the 'Resolution' under Cook and another Whitby collier of 300 tons, the 'Discovery', under Charles Clerke. Cook left England on 12 July 1776 and Clerke at the beginning of August. They met at the Cape of Good Hope and left there on 30 November 1776 sailing eastwards for the Pacific. After examining the French-discovered islands of Kergulen and Crozet, Cook went on to Tasmania. He landed there for provisions but he did not investigate whether or not it was an island. He accepted Furneaux's previous report and went on to Queen Charlotte's Sound for his fresh water, firewood and new spars, anchoring there on 12 February 1777. He now knew the true story of the Maori *massacre* of Furneaux's men but Cook refused to seek ven-

A Human Sacrifice in Tahiti, by J. Webber

geance. This was an attitude which neither the Maoris nor
Omai, the Society-islander whom Cook had aboard, could
understand.

It was now too late to hope to reach the Arctic North before
its winter set in, so Cook took a leisurely voyage to Tahiti. On
29 March he sighted new islands which later became known
as the Cook Islands and after calling at the Friendly Islands
for fresh provisions he arrived at Tahiti in August. Here he
witnessed various ceremonies, including a human sacrifice.
Cook had a long stay in these waters, taking Omai back to his
home in the Society Islands and renewing old friendships. As
the year ended Cook set sail for North America. On Christmas
Eve, 1777 he sighted and named Christmas Island and on

18 January 1778 he discovered what have come to be called the Sandwich Islands. After a short stay he let the west winds blow him to the American coast of New Albion as Drake had called it. On 7 March this coast hove into sight. He then followed the coast northwards and took his ships into Nootka Sound on Vancouver Island, though at that time Cook was not aware that it was an island. Here they traded fish and furs with the natives, leaving towards the end of April to continue their voyage north. Cook rounded the Alaskan Peninsula and then probed north into the Bering Strait until the ice blocked his way at $70\frac{1}{2}°$N. Winter was now upon him so he decided to return. The 'Resolution' was once again showing the leaks it had been prone to all the voyage, so Cook anchored at Unalaska for repairs. They were, however, only temporary and Cook decided to return to the warmth of the Sandwich Islands, there to make a proper refit.

Inside a house at Nootka Sound, by J. Webber

Man and Woman of Unalaska

Cook anchored off Hawaii, or Owhyhee as he called it, on 30 November 1778. Then for over a month he circled and surveyed the island before anchoring on the west side in Kealakekua Bay on 17 January 1779. When Cook landed he was received with great ceremony and adoration. Unbeknown to Cook the Hawaiian priests had taken him for their god Lono, who had gone away from the island long ago but who had promised his return. Cook was treated as this returning god. He was clothed in special robes, led in processions and offered a sacrificed pig. The people supplied all that Cook wanted in the way of provisions, thinking it their religious duty to supply their god with his needs. Cook was grateful for the welcome and on 4 February 1779 he left Hawaii delighted with his discovery.

Two days later they ran into a storm, the masts of the 'Resolution' were damaged and Cook decided, though with reluctance, to put back to Kealakekua Bay. This time Cook and his men were received with mixed feelings. The priests were glad to see their god but some of the chiefs and the people were reluctant to give Cook yet more provisions. There were various stone-throwing *incidents* and thefts from the sailors which came to head with the theft one night of the ship's large boat. The next day Cook decided to land with an armed party and take one of the chiefs as hostage until the boat was returned. With nine marines under Lieutenant Phillips, as escort, Cook in full uniform and carrying his double-barrelled shotgun, was rowed ashore.

The old chief when told of the theft agreed to go with Cook, but as they approached the beach two young chiefs tried to stop him by making him sit down. As a crowd grew, Cook decided that they must leave the old chief if bloodshed was to be prevented. The marines withdrew to the water's edge and as Cook followed them a native warrior made as if he was about to fling a stone at him. Cook fired one barrel of his shotgun which was loaded with small shot but it merely bounced off the warrior's shield. He came on, menacing Cook with his dagger, so Cook fired his other barrel which was loaded with

82

Ceremonial presentation of a pig to Cook, as drawn by J. Webber

Death of Cook by James Cleveley at Hawaii, Sandwich Islands is by Zoffany

ball. This time Cook killed a man. The marines also fired but the natives were not at all put off. They rushed the marines before they could reload. The men in the boats were also firing and Cook turned away from the crowd which threatened him, to call to the men in the boats to pull in. This was his undoing. While ever he faced them the natives seemed too overawed to attack him. The moment he turned his back they rushed upon him, stabbing and clubbing him as he sank to his knees in the water. Then they dragged his body ashore and butchered it.

The sailors opened fire, killing and wounding many natives. They cleared the beach but the natives dragged Cook's dead body with them, and the boats returned to the ships without him.

A few days later when tempers had cooled the sailors were allowed to have what remained of Cook's body. The natives had burnt it but it was possible to identify the remains from the scar on his hand which Cook had received when a powder flask had exploded during his voyage to Newfoundland in 1764. On 22 February 1779 Cook was buried in the bay with full naval honours.

So died Captain James Cook, R.N., the greatest explorer of the seas that the world has known. He died as he had lived, with immense courage and selflessness.

Epilogue

The expedition did not end with Cook's death. Captain Clerke continued the voyage as Cook had intended, sailing north to Petropavlovsk and into the Bering Strait from the Asiatic side. As before, the ships found their way blocked by ice and in July 1779 Clerke turned south again. He died before they could reach Petropavlovsk and Captain John Gore took command, bringing the ships back to England in October 1780.

Cook's three voyages had solved the main problems of the Pacific Ocean. In ten years he had answered questions centuries old. There was no Southern Continent, there was no North-West Passage, but there was the island continent of Australia, the two islands of New Zealand and a host of other islands, many of them explored by Cook. There was also in existence a vast amount of scientific and historical material about the islands and waters of the Pacific. The Pacific lay open—that was Captain Cook's achievement.

He adventured in those unknown seas because his curiosity drove him to find out what was really there, but those who followed him into the Pacific had different reasons for going. The British sent unwanted convicts to Australia in 1788. People hoping for a better life than that which industrial Britain gave them followed as *emigrants* to Australia and New Zealand in the nineteenth century. Whalers from Europe and America soon sought their prey and its precious oil in the Pacific, having already exterminated the whale in the Atlantic. Traders of all kinds found their way to the Pacific, dealing especially in tea, *copra* and sandalwood and later taking British cotton goods to the islands and to China. In 1819 Sir Stamford

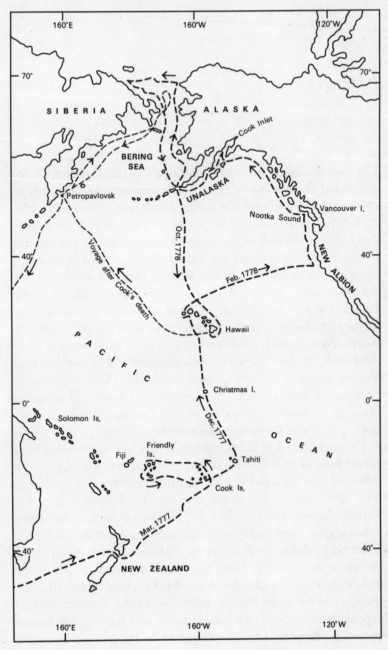

The Third Voyage of Captain Cook in the Pacific Ocean, 1776–1780

Cook Monument, Whitby

Raffles acquired Singapore on the Malay peninsula and it became the great centre for trade in the Pacific. In the north a thriving fur trade developed, especially from Nootka Sound. Slave traders, too, found both their supplies and their markets in the Pacific, for there were many tea, sugar and cotton planters to buy the natives they took off into slavery.

87

This *influx* of people into the Pacific changed the lives of its native inhabitants in ways that were not always for their good. Disease, firearms, the ills that alcohol, opium and tobacco can bring, crime and disorder—these were some of the results of the opening of the Pacific. Christian missionaries followed in the wake of the traders and emigrants and they tried to educate the islanders and reduce the ill effects which contact with western civilisation had brought. They also pressed their home governments to take over in the Pacific, to root out the criminals and the exploiters and to establish order and good government.

Gradually the governments heeded their call and assumed responsibility in the Pacific. The British had responsibility for Australia and after 1840 for New Zealand. In 1874 Britain *annexed* the Fiji Islands and a year later appointed a High Commissioner for the Western Pacific to protect the natives of the islands under British control from the ill treatment of traders. Other countries made similar annexations. In 1842 the French began to rule Tahiti and in 1853 annexed New Caledonia. In Hawaii the Americans eventually took control in 1898.

By this time the Pacific was part of the busy world at large and a highway between east and west. So much had happened since James Cook had sailed into its comparatively unknown waters in 1769.

Inscription on Cook Monument, Whitby, Yorkshire:

'For the lasting memory of a great
Yorkshire Seaman this bronze has
been cast and is left in the
keeping of Whitby, the birthplace
of those good ships that bore him
on his enterprises, brought him to
glory and left him at rest.'

Things to Do

1. Visit Whitby Museum, Yorkshire.
2. Write an imaginary letter from James Cook to his father explaining why he has decided to change his job and go to sea.
3. Find out more about the capture of Quebec 1759.
4. Imagine you were one of the crew to be 'ducked' at the Equator and write a letter to your people at home telling them about it.
5. Imagine you are a news reporter interviewing Nicholas Young (see page 44) and write an account of your interview, or record it on tape.
6. Write in diary form an account of the stay of one of the crew in Tahiti in 1769.
7. Imagine you are Omai and write a letter home comparing the life he sees in London with that he knew in the Society Islands.
8. Write an eyewitness account of the death of Cook.
9. Find out about Cook's family, draw a family tree and write an account of what happened to his children.
10. Make a book about the history of (a) Australia (b) New Zealand in the nineteenth century.

Glossary

aborigine, a primitive native found in Australia
to acclaim, to praise enthusiastically
Admiralty, the group of admirals running the navy
amateur, person who does something as a pastime
to annex, to take over another country
apprentice, learner of a craft or job
astronomy, study of the planets and stars
authentic, trustworthy
ballast, heavy material put in the hold of a ship to make it stable
Banksia, flowering plant found in Australia and New Guinea
bark, sort of ship, usually with three masts
barnacle, shell-fish that sticks to ships' bottoms
boatswain, ship's officer who looks after the rigging and calls the men
    to duty with a whistle
botany, the study of plants
brazier, pan for burning coal in
bustard, a large bird which can run very fast
calibre, ability
capstan, post which revolves and so winds in ropes or cables
careened, ship is tilted so that its bottom can be cleaned and repaired
caulking, making a ship watertight by plugging seams with pitch
collier, ship used to carry coal
to commission, to appoint as an officer in the navy
comptroller, man in charge of expenditure on ships
consistence, degree of thickness
contiguous, next to
continent, large area of land
copper, iron or copper boiler
copra, dried coconut kernels
cutter, fast sailing ship with one mast
to defray, to cover a cost by payment
to dissect, to cut up a fish or animal to examine it in detail
90   *draught*, depth of water that a ship needs to float

eclipse, when the moon passes between the earth and the sun and cuts out some of the sunlight

efficacy, degree of success

emigrant, someone who leaves one country to live permanently in another

entrails, inner part of an animal

epileptic, person who has a disease of the brain which causes fits

equinoctial, the equator, imaginary line around the middle of the earth

fathom, measure of six feet

fearnought, strong woollen cloth used for clothing

fictitious, imaginary, not real

fillet, cloth band worn round the head

folio, large sort of book in which the papers are folded only once

forfeit, payment made instead of doing some action

fumigation, disinfecting a place by smoking it out with fumes from a fire

galley, ship's kitchen

grapeshot, cannon shell made up of many small balls and designed to scatter when fired

gratification, payment

hawseholes, holes in bows through which anchor cables run

hold, space below ship's deck for cargo

impressment, forcing men to service in the navy

incidents, occasions

inferior, lower in position or knowledge

influx, crowding in

inimitable, so excellent that it is difficult to imitate or copy it

insatiable, never satisfied, always wanting to know more

landscape, scenery or view

lead, lump of metal dropped on a line into the water to tell its depth

llama, animal of South America, like a camel but without a hump

marine biology, the study of plant life in the sea

massacre, killing everybody in the party

memorial, written document

minerals, substances obtained from the earth by mining, like coal or diamonds

parallel, imaginary line marking a degree of latitude

phaenomenon, (modern spelling: phenomenon) an event of scientific interest

pease, peas

peninsula, piece of land almost surrounded by water

pike, a pointed metal weapon mounted on the end of a wooden shaft

pinnace, large boat, usually eight-oared

profusion, great number

puncheon, large cask

quadrant, instrument for measuring angles and heights

Quaker, member of a religious sect which believes in plain ways of life

quarto, sort of book in which the pages are folded twice

to redress, to put right

repugnant, against, in opposition to

reved, threaded through

sentiments, opinions

sheathe, cover

shoals, submerged sand-banks

sounded, tested to find the depth of the water

spars, poles used for masts and to support sails

stowages, spaces

swivel, gun on pivot allowing it to rotate

tolerant, able to understand other people

towsers, an old sort of trousers, made out of coarse material

transit, passing over

victuals, food, provisions

void, empty

wainscote, wooden panelling of wall of a room

windlass, machine for hoisting or hauling with a rope which winds round a cylinder

yawl, small boat with four to six oars